July 13. 1998
In loving memory
of Georgie.

Clarie

The
Tree
That
Survived
the
Winter

by
Mary Fahy

Illustrated by

Emil Antonucci

Paulist Press
New York/Mahwah, N.J.

Text copyright © 1989 by Mary Fahy.

Illustrations copyright © 1989 by Emil Antonucci.

Library of Congress Cataloging-in-Publication Data

Fahy, Mary. 1938–
    The tree that survived the winter/by Mary Fahy.
        p.   cm.
    Summary: A tree survives the cold winter in this parable about the power of faith.
    ISBN 0-8091-0432-6
    1. Parables.   2. Christian life—Catholic authors.
[1. Parables.   2. Christian life.]   I. Title.
BV4515.2.F34   1989
242—dc20   89-37972
                                                                        CIP
                                                                          AC

Published by Paulist Press
997 Macarthur Boulevard
Mahwah, New Jersey 07430

Printed and bound in the
United States of America

To Claire
whose fidelity to her own inner journey
inspired this story.

The tree awakened earlier than usual one morning and stretched her arms toward the horizon as if to invite the early rays of dawn into her world. She shivered with delight, wiggling her roots in the muddy earth, which had only recently yielded its frozen hardness.

She sensed something was different. Her roots seemed to be extending further and more firmly into the soil. Her arms seemed to embrace more of the world, not with the timid gestures of a sapling afraid of tangling with the wind, but with the freedom of knowing that the wind could not topple her.

"I have survived the winter!" she marveled aloud.

"How wonderful," whispered the dawn, who had a facility for appreciating new miracles no matter how often they occurred. She swirled around the young tree in a ritual of blessing, enveloping her gently, making her feel very special.

"How very different this feels," mused the tree, for a few short weeks ago the melting earth beneath her roots had sent shivers of panic through every single branch. She had cried out in alarm then, sensing that she might sink into that dark hole and lose herself.

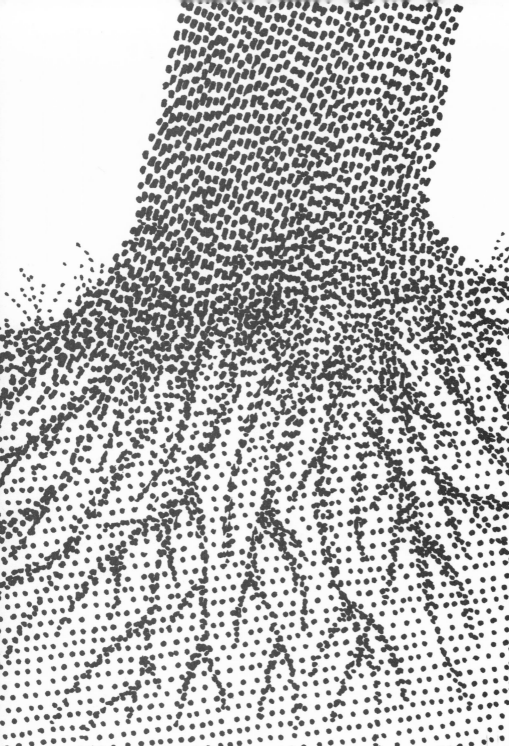

"How silly it all seems now," she realized, but the feelings had been real and could not be denied.

It was not unlike the despair she had experienced earlier, when she had been removed from her safe and comfortable nursery bed and transplanted to this lonely hillside. She vividly recalled how frightened she had been, so isolated from all that was familiar and precious to her, so trapped in her fear, so unsure of who she was and what was to become of her.

But mingled with the fear had been that saving, undeniable sense that she had been chosen from among others, had been transplanted with love and conviction to this spot.

Often during the cold winter she had questioned the reason, but even while she had trembled with anxiety she had felt an inner voice—a small but steady voice—which remained fluid and alive when everything else in her had seemed paralyzed.

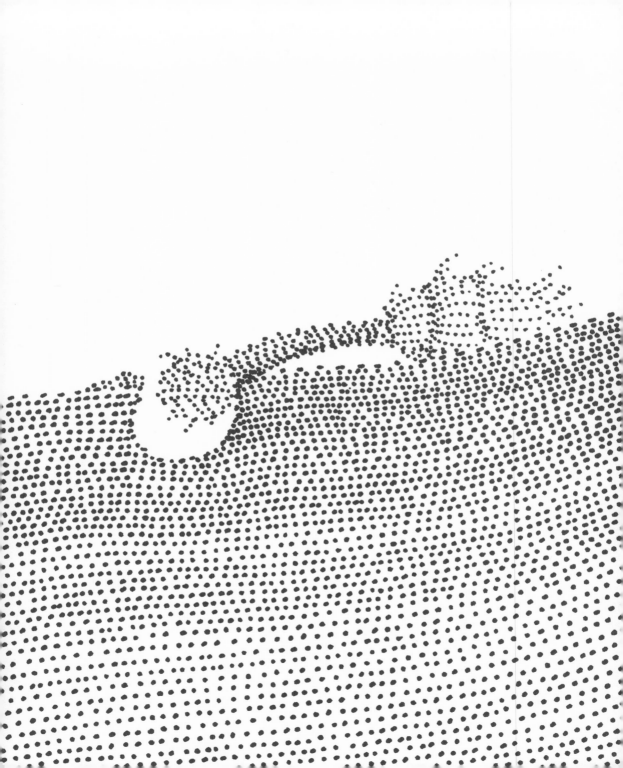

But now—*now!*—she was filled with the realization that her inner life was in harmony with the world outside. She relaxed the tight fibers of her being which she had unwittingly held rigid during the cold gray months.

"I have survived the winter!" she exulted.

"You have survived the winter!" the birds echoed, hopping eagerly from branch to branch, bouncing on the tender extensions of herself that the tree had not even noticed.

"Oh!"

This one word, spoken softly and reverently, was all the tree could manage as she examined the white buds beginning to show through the tips of her branches, once held hard-clenched against the winter winds.

"I have survived the winter," the tree sighed, "and I have grown!"

"You have survived the winter and you have grown," chorused the breezes that tickled her gently and sent her dancing to their syncopated rhythm.

Days passed, and the energy within her fairly exploded, spilling out into clusters of lovely blossoms. She watched each day as they grew larger and more beautiful.

Spring rains showered her with congratulations and encouragement. "You have survived the winter and you are growing, growing, growing . . ."

"Growing! Yes, I am growing," the tree acknowledged. "I have survived the winter and I am growing." She shivered with delight as she admired her new appearance, letting a few raindrops fall on the violets that enjoyed the shelter of her trunk. "It is good to be alive," she told them.

"Growing! Yes, I am growing," the tree acknowledged. "I have survived the winter and I am growing." She shivered with delight as she admired her new appearance, letting a few raindrops fall on the violets that enjoyed the shelter of her trunk. "It is good to be alive," she told them.

"Indeed," said the sun, appearing suddenly from behind a rain cloud, "you have survived the winter because you are very much loved!"

The tree could feel the warmth of the smiling sun penetrate deep into her branches, even through the bark of her trunk. She stood up tall and proud as if for inspection.

"I am rather lovely, aren't I?" she asked, giving a casual rustle to her blossoms and a graceful curtsey with her boughs. "See how well I have survived the winter."

But then she stopped.

For the memory of the hard winter sent through her a stab of anger and pain that she thought the spring had healed.

"Where were you when I needed you?" she cried to the sun, and suddenly her pent-up anguish found release in a flow of fluid that oozed from the cracks in her bark and trickled down the sides of her trunk.

"I needed you! I needed you so badly and you weren't there," she sobbed. "You've been gone so long, and I've been so cold and lonely and scared. The days were so gray when you weren't here, and even when I could see you in the distance I couldn't feel your warmth or seem to reach you with my voice. Didn't you see me shivering? I became so brittle I was afraid of breaking, and my roots became paralyzed in the earth, and my bark cracked open, and . . ."

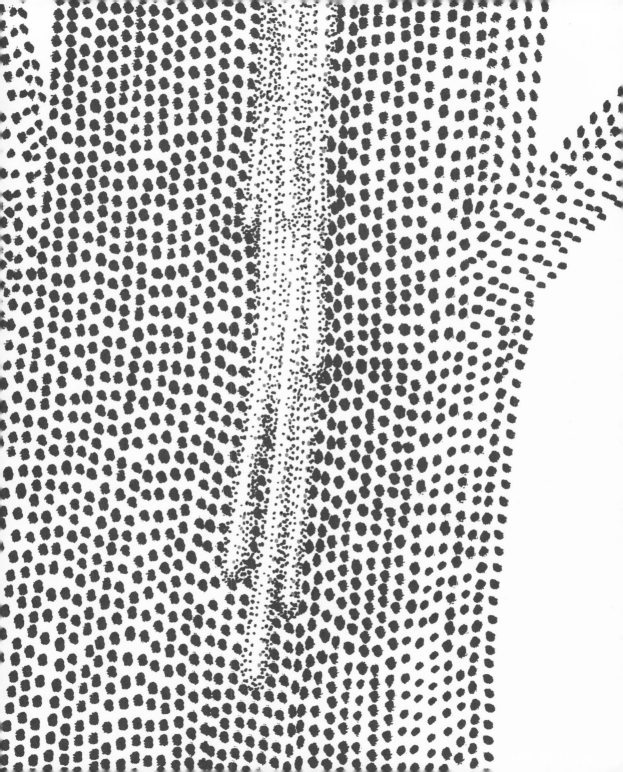

She could no longer go on except to cry out:
". . . and I *missed* you—terribly!"

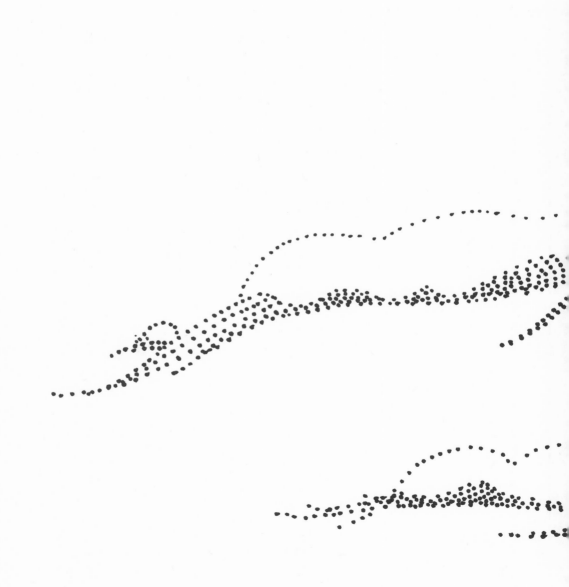

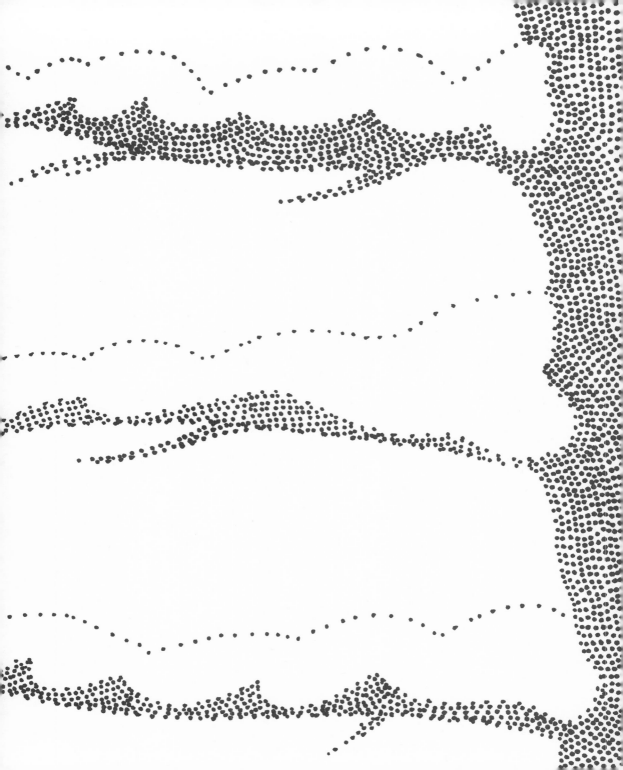

The sun's glow only intensified and the message was repeated. "You have survived the winter because you are very much loved."

"Loved?" She hesitated, not wanting to challenge the statement but needing to be reassured.

"It's true," replied the sun, "that there were days when the clouds seemed to separate us, but I was really there, even when you couldn't see me. And those days when I was visible but remote—when you couldn't feel my warmth—those were the days when I sent a concentration of light. Why, there were even times when I gave you light and snow at the same time so that my brightness would be reflected up at you as well as shining down. Those were the days when you thought the glare was too strong, the light was too bright. You were seeing more than you wanted to see. Remember?"

The tree stood dumbfounded.

The sun continued. "The chills and ice and bitter cold have toughened your timber to just the right degree, for you needed to be strong to carry the fruit that will appear on your branches. If I had stayed close all winter, you would not have grown this strong. In fact, you could not have become at all what I hoped and dreamed you would be. But now—just look at you!"

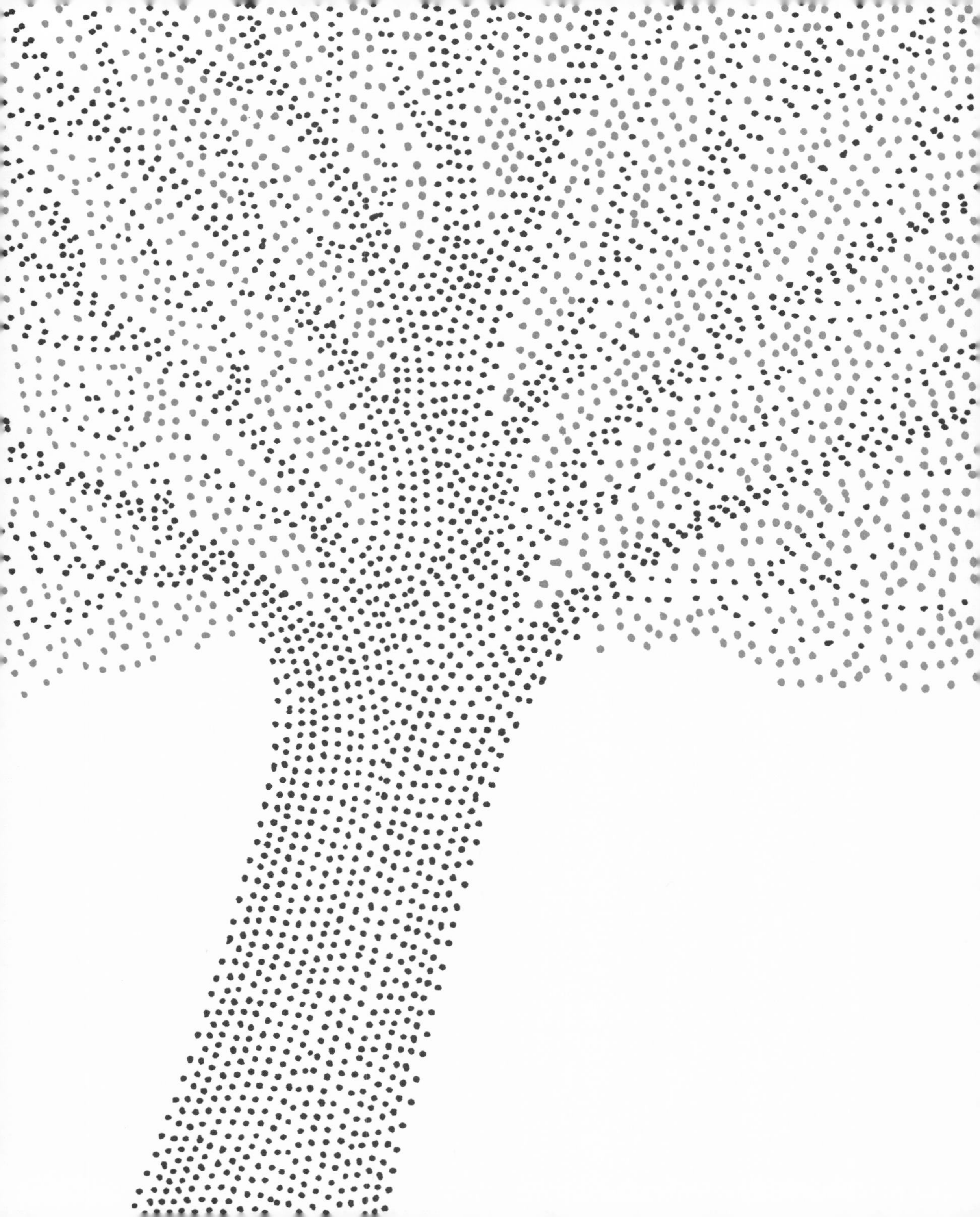

A blush of pink coursed through her petals. The tree stood speechless.

"You have survived the winter because you are, and were, and always will be very much loved," said the sun. "For that small place deep within you that remained unfrozen and open to mystery, that is where I have made my dwelling. And long, long before you felt my warmth surrounding you, you were being freed and formed from within in ways so deep and profound that you could not possibly know what was happening."

"I . . . I . . . I believed," she whispered, noticing that the words seemed to come from that inner space deep within her.

"Yes, you have believed," sparkled the sun. "You have always believed, and that is what enabled you to grow. For had you not kept faith with me in the center of your being, you could not have blossomed into you."

This was almost too much joy for the tree to bear. She raised her arms high in praise, but no words would come, and no words were necessary.

Weeks passed and the once-lonely tree became a part of life in the meadow. She playfully caught the kites of the children who gathered nearby, and then in a spirit of fair play tossed them back again.

"You are a good sport," they said to her. "We will call you Friend."

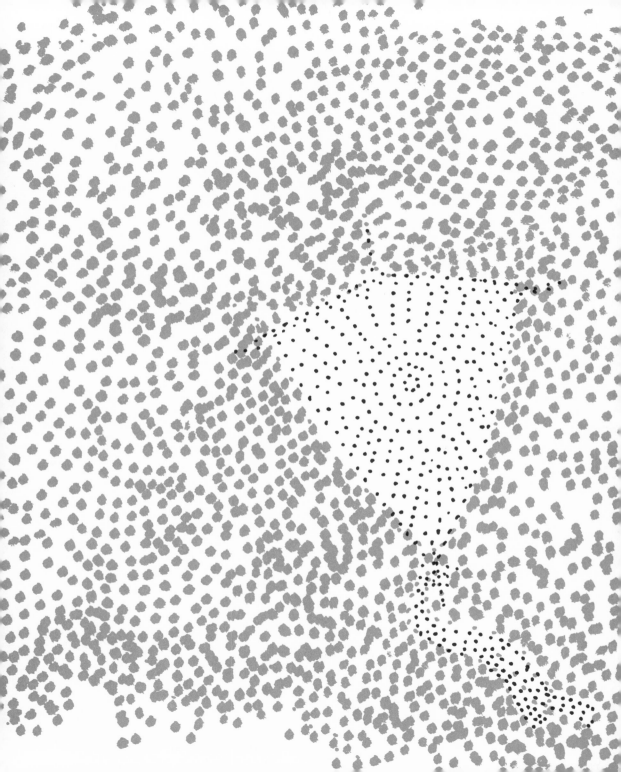

A young couple sat beneath the shade of her thickening leaves and spoke of their love for each other. "This is a special place," they said, and they left their initials carved next to her heart.

"We shall call you Keeper of Secrets," they said to her.

A tired, troubled woman, bent with care, walked silently through the meadow, oblivious to everything except her own worries. She did not even notice the tree.

"Come and rest a while," whispered the tree, but she had to toss a piece of fruit onto the path before the woman saw her. Wearily, the woman sat, and ate the fruit, and pondered deeply. The tree could feel the woman relax as she rested against her trunk.

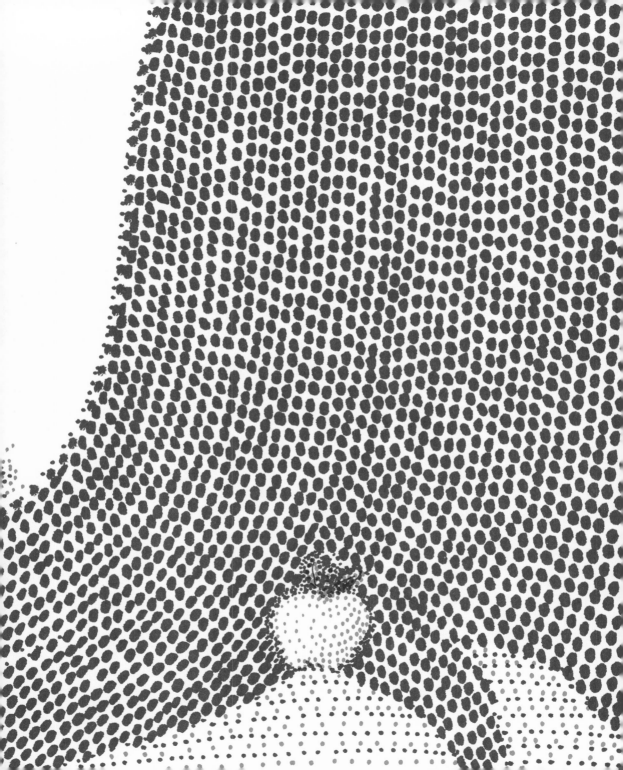

Finally the woman stood up. "Thank you," she murmured and embraced the tree.

The tree winced, for the woman had touched a spot that had not healed from the winter's ravages—a spot that remained vulnerable though the spring and summer months had been good to her. The woman seemed to notice and caressed the spot thoughtfully. At that moment there was a oneness—a sense of understanding between the troubled woman and the tree.

"I will call you Hope," whispered the woman, and touched her again with affection and gratitude.

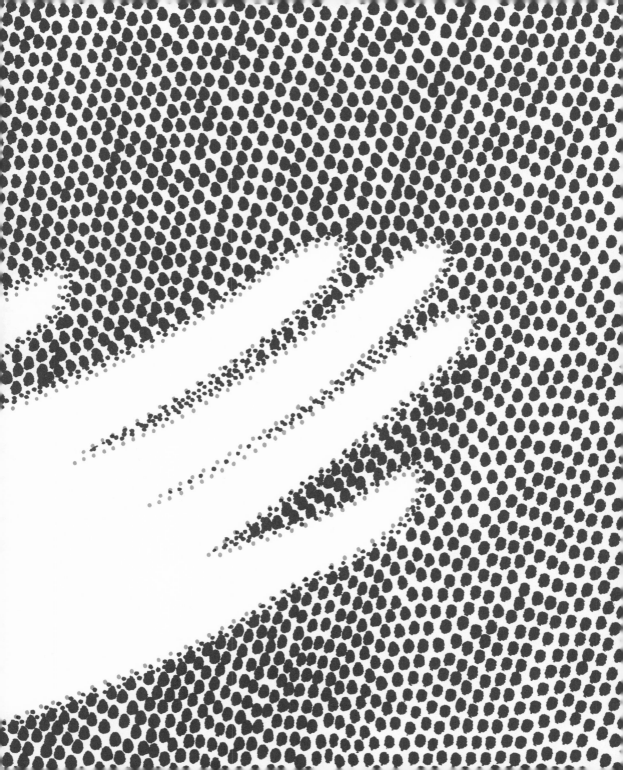

Profoundly humbled, the tree bent low,
grateful for the obvious gifts she had to share,
but even more grateful for the less obvious—the
scars that produced an unspeakable solidarity.

Long after her fruit had been shared and she began noticing touches of scarlet in her leaves, the tree still carried deep within her the memories of all her experiences.

"Who could possibly have imagined all that has happened to me?" she said to no one in particular.

And then, addressing herself to the sun, she said, ". . . except you!"

"Have you seen? Have you heard?" she asked eagerly. "I am needed! I am wanted! I am sharing life at a whole new level. And best of all, I am named. Aren't they beautiful names? I am called Friend, and Keeper of Secrets, and Hope."

"Indeed," replied the sun, splashing a smile across the evening sky. "And what is the name I have given you?"

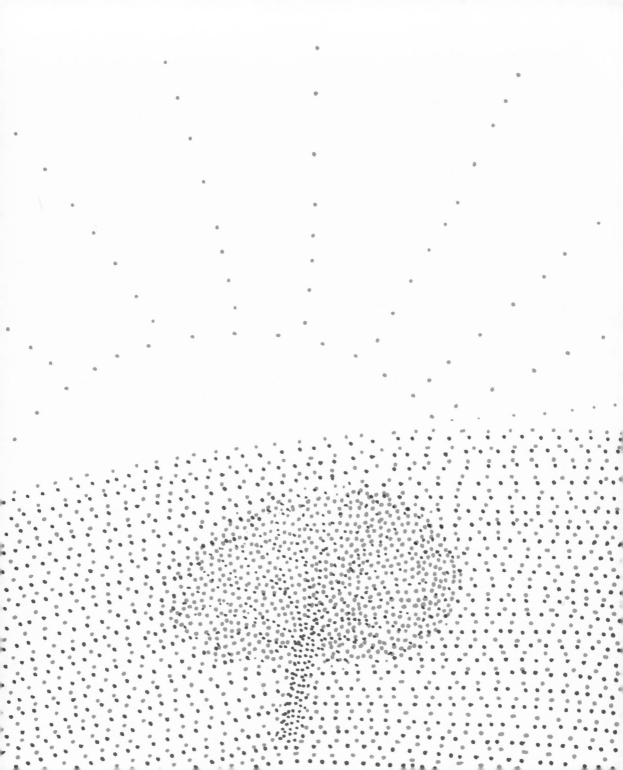

"You have named me?" the tree asked, astonished at her lack of awareness.

"Long before you were a seedling," the sun replied solemnly.

"What do you call me?" she asked.

"Stay with the question," the sun answered. "And listen very, very carefully and I will tell you."

Watching the sun slide behind the farthest hill, she stood motionless, waiting in the promise of the newly-painted sky.

"What do you call me?" she asked again in the stillness of the night.

"You are called Faithful," said the small voice from within.

"You are called Faithful," blinked the evening star, as if to reassure her.

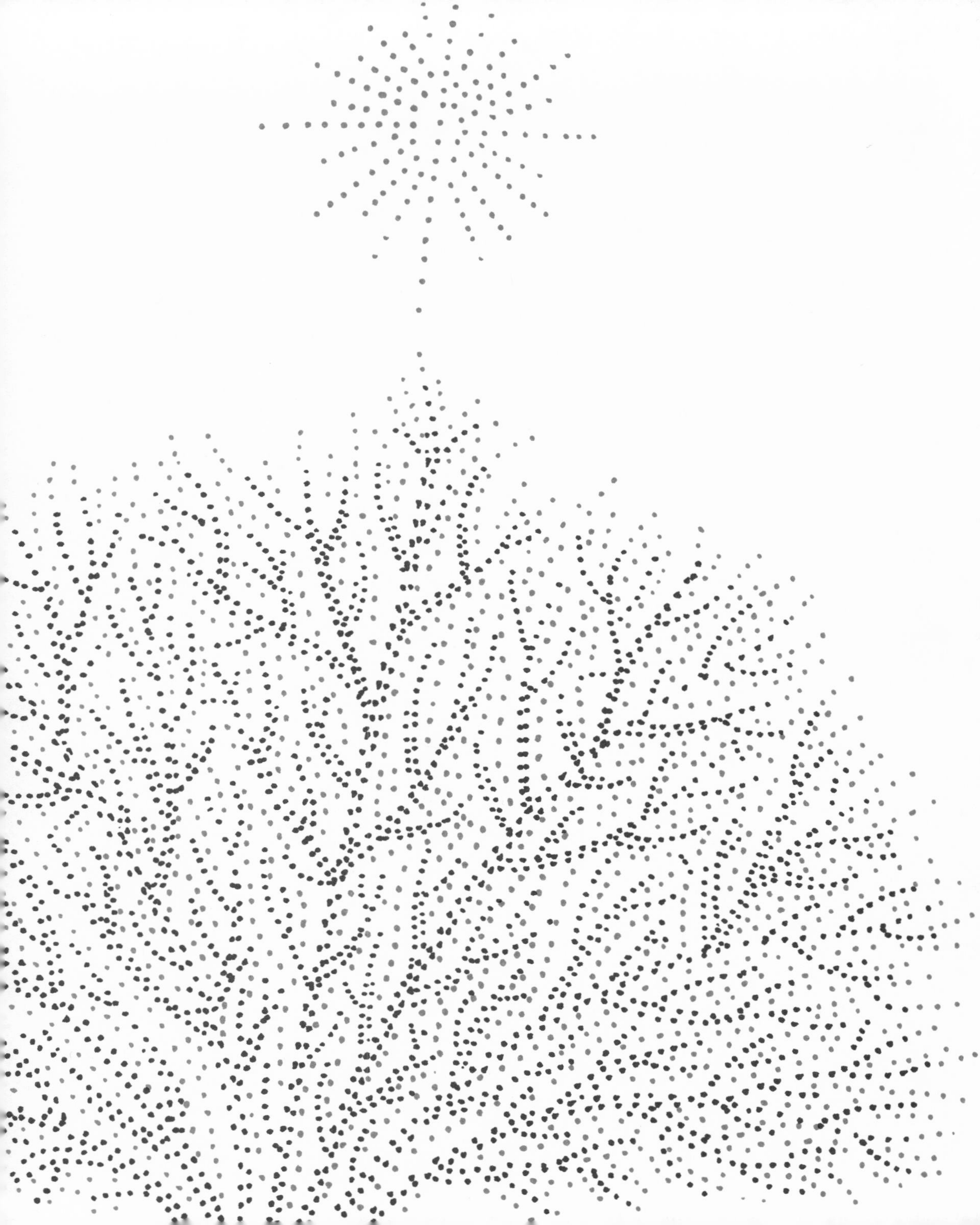

"Y ou are called Faithful," proclaimed a trillion other stars as they burst through the darkness of the night.